Ann Gadd proudly uncorks

Wine a bit and
Ewe will feel better

Gateway Publishing Limited
PO Box 2031 – Sark – GY10 1PB – Channel Islands
Telephone: +44 (0)1865 723404
www.gatewaysark.co.uk
email: info@gatewaysark.co.uk

ISBN 978-1-902471-08-2

Wine a bit and
Ewe will feel better

Rickety Bridge
P.O. Box 455
Franschhoek
7690

Tel: +27 (0) 21 876 2129
Fax: +27 (0) 21 876 3486
Info@ricketybridge.com

Ann Gadd is one of South Africa's most popular and best-selling artists.

In 1997 after a career in advertising and design, Ann began to indulge her passion for painting more seriously, becoming a full-time artist and author.

In early 2002 she painted her first 'ewe' painting. The painting sold as did three further similarly styled works, but it was not until 2006 that she took the concept further creating the style of work for which she has become well known.

She has participated in a large number of group and solo exhibitions and her paintings hang in collections both locally and internationally.

In a world where little is new, her quirky, humorous, yet insightful art is both fresh and unique. A vibrant and prolific artist, she is also the author of 11 published books.

The Story of Ewe

Ewe was tired of having the wool pulled over her eyes. Working for a large corporate flock in the *Maa*keting Department, she discovered she was being fleeced by those with more R.A.M.

Her stock options were limited to either being roast lamb or someone's new sweater.

Neither was appealing.

So she decided to see if the grass was greener on the other side, and, telling them to flock off, (in the nicest possible way), she set off to find the real ewe. At times she felt like a lost sheep and had to do several *ewe*turns until she found the path to creating her own *ewe*nique art. Since then she has found *ewe*topia.

Her paintings form part of collections in *Ewe*rope, the *Ewe*.K. the *Ewe*.S.A. and many other parts of the world.

Being a wine *connoshear*, collaborating with Rickety Bridge Winery to produce this series, has been another exciting development in her artistic career.

A lively white with a delightful
bouquet

4

A toast to ewe!

Aromatic with earthy aftertaste

Baachus

Baaman

Box Wine

Chenin Blaanc and Cabaanet

Coarse but generous...

Cult wines

Dark and seductive...

Dracewela

Flabby and faded...

Flocking good wine

Full-bodied yet lacks finesse

Greenpeppers on the nose

Here's to ewe!

Horizontal wine tasting

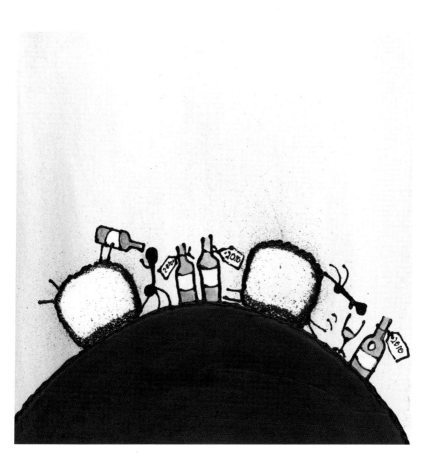

Lacks concentration

Lamb marinated in red wine

Liquid Assets

Noble Late Harvest

Raising the Baa

Robust with barnyard character

Rolling with the Punches

Rosemary stuffed lamb in red wine

Sabaage

54

A short finish

Spring lamb with white wine

Tannin

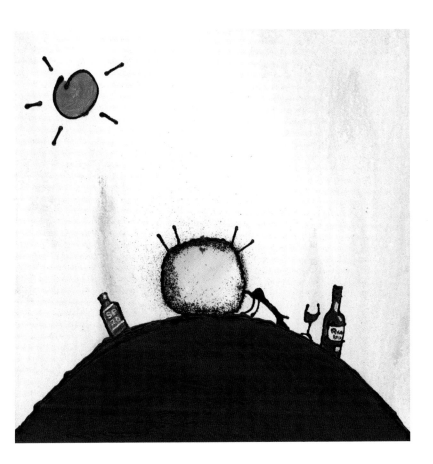

Tart and quite forward...

Under the Weather

Vertical wine tasting

Well balanced

Wine Menewe

The wine went straight to my head

The Wine Baa

Winos ewephemism: three sheeps to
the wind

76

With each glass of wine ewe became
more intelligent

78